War Diary

Susan M. Schultz

SPUYTEN DUYVIL
New York City

ISBN 978-1-969900-13-6

for Yaroslava Antipina

@strategywoman

Open Door Policy

2 March 2022

—We will keep the door open, says the diplomat.
—We will keep the door open, says the president.
—We will keep the door open, says the tyrant.
—We will keep the door open, says the border guard.
—We will keep the door open, says the chef.

Babushka, in dark coat and cap, clutches anti-nuclear signs almost as tall as she is. One Darth Vader stands at each of her elbows; they lean over. Each Vader takes one of her arms. She doesn't drop her signs.

He says he cannot post the video. It's too horrible. So he describes it.

Old woman toe to toe with Russian soldier. She talks to him about sunflowers, but she doesn't put one inside the muzzle of his gun.

Column of Russian tanks meets column of unarmed Ukrainians. Traffic jam as resistance.

Bright lemons hang in front of a blue house. Bright yellow strip on telephone pole beneath blue sky. Blue wooden support beam meets yellow at the site of a torn spider web. (That photograph lost to digital hash.)

She sees balance in her being on 1) a Russian to-kill list, and 2) Ukrainian top 10 Bachelorette.

"Fuck you, Russian ship."

What have I done to stop the war today? Eaten my cereal. Taken my walk. Sat down under ʻōhiʻa's bird canopy to type. Years ago, I got a call at 3 a.m. to tell me that my mother had fallen down.

Her elbow was broken, but her bones were too fragile to set.

—We will keep the door open.

What says the door?

How to Talk about Bad Stuff

4 March 2022

He sits at the end of a long, narrow table. Men in suits sit at the other end, but we can't see them yet. One road over, Tibetan flags hang in a vacant but well-tended lot, wet, on strings. Blue and yellow masks gaze from ‘ōhi‘a trees. One is wrapped in wire, face a cipher. Another has a long ceramic chin, bent like a banana. A horse strides across one flag, through which light blurs. From close-up, language turns to wires hanging between trees.

He wraps his girlfriend in newspaper after a shower. On her belly the headline about a man who killed his three year old and then himself. It's not wet enough not to be legible. It's not legible enough to grieve.

Lilith goes chin to chin with a pink flamingo beside a small tree. Label in front of flamingo reads "lime."

The oligarch's 600 million dollar yacht was not taken, but

it's not allowed to leave the harbor of Hamburg. Plus it has maintenance issues. Some sanctions are accidents.

I have a hard time reading the computer's small print. I'm told I have a "good eye."

Is that a civil defense test in Volcano or an air raid siren in Kyiv? Is the television on or off?

The affect of reading her perhaps out-weighs its content, which is not to say the content isn't embedded in our time, like a reporter in a tank in Iraq, or the man who tweets out each morning that he's alive in the Ukraine. This is not a criticism: I feel her words' import, always in conjunction with the time. The screen on my camera reads "cleaning contacts" and shivers, at least when the digital screen works. Otherwise, look through the narrow tunnel of the view finder to compose what has already been composed. To compose in this case is to frame, and to frame is to turn time into space. He took photos that made the earth stop, sun moving across it.

Each camera has its own eye. I compose according to its eye, as much as my own. Bryant has cleared one camera's lens; no more black blobs on blue sky. If you look at the sky past the yellow diamond "No exit" sign, you see a Ukrainian flag.

How to talk to your kids about Ukraine. How to talk to your kids about child sexual abuse. How to talk to your kids about gender identity. How to talk to your kids about being canceled. How to talk to your kids about bullying, the toll it takes on their mental health. How to talk to your daughter about the soccer player who killed herself. She's been on a suicide watch (not her own), so she knows.

"I hope I was not too forward."

War Diary

8 March 2022

A woman on twitter invites you to share "war coffee" with her in Kyiv. She's abandoned make-up, but still drinks coffee each morning, sharing occasional selfies without the smile. The soccer player who died by suicide smiled for hers. Obligatory happiness. Her mother wears her daughter's sweatshirt. Smell is presence, not pretense.

I took pictures of a black & white photo of my father. When I turned the photo around and put it at the window, I could still see him, along with the name of the studio in Alexandria, Virginia. There's no sentiment to the image; it was a head shot for work. Mid to late 1960s? He's not smiling, and he's wearing a suit and tie. But as I carry him from window to tree and from tree to blue bowl and from bowl to the orange-speckled chair on the porch, I talk to him about war. On the Washington Mall, a plane flew over, low, and he said, "Imagine if they were shooting at us."

I placed him on the reflective silver ball in the crook of a hapu`u fern, and pushed the shutter. His image appeared to melt into ferns, taffied by memory.

When I took a photo of his photo, showing just one eye and the edge of his mouth, he looked like Eisenhower.

President Zelenskyy speaks to his phone in a square full of sand bags. He talks softly, so as not to alert his enemies. It's the beginning of Spring in Kyiv, and he's outdoors in his drab green shirt and jacket. He repeats words. This is how we know he's rhetorically brilliant. And then he winks.

Is that a selfie? Or a war-time speech to his own device, held out for the benefit of Instagram and Facebook? A grandmother falls by the train tracks and two soldiers pick her up.

To each our war diary; it's the new democracy of affect. A friend vomited in her sleep, she's so troubled by her television. Another friend wants to volunteer with Sean Penn, doesn't know that Penn left his film behind. To watch is to act, isn't it?

The man in gray pony tale said he laughs at tourists because they wear watches, consult them frequently. My empty wrist, to say nothing of my dog, assures him I'm not a tourist. Says vaccinations should be the individual's choice, and besides don't people still get covid?

My father's on the coffee table now, staring up awkwardly in his suit and tie. I walk past him many times a day. My photo project's done, and he was well received. May his memory be a blessing.

Tweeting Woman

11 March 2022

Erased yesterday's entry and changed the date. A Ukrainian woman on twitter can't find a manicure. "Do you not know people are dying?" is one man's response. Does he not know the value of nails neatly trimmed, of the clothes we work in and those we sleep in? (Sometimes they're the same.) Each nail marks a boundary between air and skin, a mobile defense system to keep us in our chairs. She hasn't left her home, sends photos of coffee cups, steaming.

I join her for coffee, laughing at her previously-annoying neighbors, Snoring Man and Sneezing Man. I once lived next door to Laughing Man.

Atrocity as cliché. Russian soldiers talk to their wives on their phones. One is bringing back a large TV, another a kitchen appliance his wife requested. Another says they shot two civilians who saw them. There's less bluster in opposing war, sticking a hole in your gas tank and walking away. Four soldiers confront an elderly couple. She shoos them away like stray geese.

Dear Y: It's a cool, crisp morning in Volcano, Hawai`i. I'm in a rain forest, listening to birds, tracing the course of shadows through the large leaves and the hapu`u fronds. My dog Lilith got loose yesterday and ran through the forest chasing pheasants. When I came around a corner and saw her at the end of the loop, I called her name. She turned, ran the other way with an absolute joy I can't deny her. When she returned, it was for water. This story escapes allegory; it's much more simple than that. The dog in my former student's film was beautiful in this way, walking an old man toward his death, tail up, nose out for the ghost of the old man's wife under the tree outside.

Our suffering over your suffering hardly matters. My writing to your writing is trivial. Our despair kills only us. The man's grief over his wife's miscarriage isn't sentiment; it's analogue. Witness doesn't abide scale. I'm writing words as if to protect you from bullets and bombs. A comedian speaks for us all.

#War Coffee

14 March 2022

Watched *Winter on Fire* last night. History has an inside, like the cave of the heart, or spleen. "They are not human beings," human beings kept saying about other human beings. Broken things: buildings, noses, eyes, the voices of witnesses. History broken, like a skull. A wounded soldier holds up his phone in bed and Zelenskyy enters his selfie. Gives the man a medal.

Bird song, until the television comes on to sirens, explosions. Not better to be there, but better to feel a part of it, to have a hand to lend, to be a witness with benefits (as it were). The screen is a part in information's skull. You can be arrested in Russia for trading information.

You don't fuck with Ukrainians. Bodies against tanks. Bodies against trucks. Bodies against Darth Vaders with steel wands, their magic the fracturing of bodies. They want to be more like us. Decadent, corrupt, possessed of the courage not to wear a cloth mask.

Yesterday, Lilith escaped again. Across the road, inside dense rain forest foliage, I heard pheasants being flushed this way, then that. Punctuated by barks. She came toward me; when I called, she re-entered the forest. She came back when she got thirsty.

There's drama without plot. An explosion ends development, gets too quickly to denouement, kills the syllogism. Death is not a plot, nor is it an endpoint. The street-fighting continues, a young man telling his mother on the phone that he loves her (because he's so prompted). A body lies 10 feet away.

How do I spend my creative time? a friend asks. Very poorly. What is to be made against the vision of so much unmaking? I don't see babushkas screaming at Russian soldiers any more, just stretchers spat out from a hospital. The journalist says his colleague was shot and left behind. He says that from his cot.

I've started reading Yoko Ogawa's *The Memory Police* again, though I hardly ever re-read. It's about forgetting the plot, the objects that populate it. It's about erasure. If we are mandated to forget, we also forget to care for. A stray bird means nothing. The narrator's mother has kept some forgotten objects, like perfume, in her furniture. After their death, they are magical in resurrection. The ordinary is what becomes sacred after its objects are forgotten. A manicure in war-time is act of resistance. Let's drink more war coffee across our twitter feeds.

Mirror Stage

15 March 2022

So much is about watching suffering you can't touch. Where's the virtual hand for touching the virtual head of a woman on a stretcher? Is prayer an artificial hand? Do I lift my mug of war coffee with a prayer, not a fist? We have to say our mantras, John High writes, but I don't know which to say.

Dear Y, we both drink morning coffee, take morning walks. We both want to be safe. I don't want a manicure, but you do; I'd prefer a massage. You take pictures out your window in the morning, as do I. If my window could see your window, we might catch each other's eyes. They're good eyes. But twitter is all the eye we have now. I find your noun-verb issues moving.

See Me, Feel Me

24 March 2022

What you do when you can't touch. The mask between mouth and supermarket air.

What is most ordinary gains power because we can hope to touch it. Harsh texture of hand-made paper, neat flex of a pocket knife, soft remnant wasp nest, a green newsboy cap. The tool puts you back together as it takes a machine apart. Paper can't accommodate writing, except recycled words trapped inside it.

She writes through her twitter mask, from her twitter handle, posting a photograph from her window each morning. Perfect for an "uninteresting photographs" site, except we know it's in Ukraine. There are no shelled apartment blocks, no burned cars, no sheeted bodies. The scene, while dull, is oddly, miraculously alive. Except our air is not hers. Her air is symbolic, while ours is just the wind that shook our cottage last night, brought trees into speech. Memory is another word for it.

The loss of the poet is real, though I only met him once. The loss of a girl in the Ukraine is only image, or news report. Transpose the grief you can touch onto a more abstract grieving. That might end a war or two, no?

A church sign down Highway 11 reads: "When the world is cray cray / Jesus is the way way." Underneath, ads for therapy and food. Half of all college students suffer the lack of a basic need, and this new 3-year plan will address that lack with food and new administrators. The strategic plan stands in for care; it's the absence of touch that promises touch.

The screen reflects, but it also divides, like a wall. We will keep you out by looking at you. Witness promises some kind of touch, but watching does not. I will sit with it. I will live with the poem inside my head for years. I will make of my skull space a haven, bomb shelter, community center. There is nothing private about our heads; it's the gallery of our public imagining, and you go there to look at it.

My meditations are as abstract as they want not to be. What I touch is keyboard, and the cool wind brushes my shoulders. The window in front of me frames ferns, living and dead, through which the morning sun travels. A spider's thread glints between leaf and wiry trunk. Bryant said a small bird was hanging upside down from the gutter looking for spiders. Yes, the film was very slow, but when I woke up the next day, I had been in it.

The New Normal

25 March 2022

Possessives. Your war is not my war, but I share it somehow. I write in parallel. Your time shattered, mine still a thread, if a bit bare. "Who would read this?" she asked. Resistance in the micro-narrative.

One woman says there is no normal; to say "normal" is to actively forget those for whom such a thing never exists. Another wants normal life inside her war, makes coffee in the morning and evening, looks out her window, counts the internal refugees.

Tony's student asks if I simply write my sentences, or if I take weeks to put them together. I tell his class that, while I'm hardly Emerson, I believe the poems are all out there, and we walk into them, take them down not in the sense of taking down a building but in that of penciling them into speech. If you want to tell a story later, you can't afford to judge.

Seven Russian generals dead, a battalion commander killed by his own troops. A tank ran over him. You're in a foreign place, though you have a common language. You've been sent there to depopulate it, degrade it, set up a Commissioner of Despair. But it turns out you've been had. He'd known some dark mothers. And you are they.

This is my war by proxy. Rather, I am *your* proxy, permitted the space to think on it. I've had my morning coffee, walked Lilith, thought of you and your son in your small village outside Kyiv. We haven't lost normal so much as discovered how to make it.

Stop Time

27 March 2022

Strategy woman, the one who lives next door to Snoring Man, tweets today's photo out of her window. We see through it, too often without seeing *it*. Not the frame but the panes.

This morning, dementia comes up over and again. The world is crazy, my correspondent says. It's only apt, this repetition of the process of losing, mind and body, identity and mass. If we are not our identities, we change less when we lose our minds. She resembled my mother, which meant that she was. There's some use for images in this life.

Photo is marker, not anchor, like us. We wander the length of our tape measure and then we're gone. The tape measure ripped to shreds, we lose place in our own time. It ceases to matter how much we've lived, because we can't remember the thread. A life not of seasons but of gun shots, not of gentle repetition, but of ends that mean nothing.

Russia calls for the surrender of Mariupol, which they've

destroyed. "I want to get the fuck out," a Russian soldier says to his grandmother on the phone.

The nightmare is double, like eyes that don't see straight, or see two things that blur together, as if we'd put on the wrong glasses. She changed her meds, remembers her dreams now. Most of them are nightmares. Another friend dreamed over and over of having to flee. "This really happened," Ginsberg prophesied.

The cadence of his speech. He talks to us through phone, across space, in his time, and ours, which are not the same. Our time pretends to ribbon on, day to follow day to follow some notion of there being a history to be recorded. His shatters, though the lens of his phone still coheres. He still speaks in sentences, those that echo and repeat, laud and chastise. We know the sorrow of sentences destroyed.

There is too much loss, the Black dharma teacher said, for us to have the time to grieve. We start, and we start, and we start, but we can't come to the end of it before another man is shot dead by police, and another Ukrainian woman finds her son dead on the street. Time accelerates; grieving cannot.

Theater of War

28 March 2022

A old man and an old woman walk through a destroyed town in the Ukraine. They say Ukrainians destroyed the town to pretend Russians had. War as put-on, every act the last act of a tragedy. You believe it, even if you see it.

Is war the ultimate form of not-knowing, or the opposite? We're Kantians, Carla tells me, though I hardly know what that means. Perhaps we crave consistency: thought and feeling, the deer and the dachsund. We want suffering to make us think better, and thinking to help us feel. The chain gang starts to sing.

Photo Without Person

30 March 2022

The cave of the heart is mist-full this morning. Wistful in an underexposed way. There's more information in a dark photograph than in a bright one, so I make clouds dim, ocean dim, and spinner dolphins spin out of focus. What was intended as cross-species portrait is a blurry splash of sea water beyond a crabbed tree, clinging to a lava rock. Mustard gold lichen, cleft in the black rock, as to my right a woman throws a ball into the water for her one dog, and then the other. The first dog drops the ball before getting to the slippers she points to; the ball starts to roll back toward the water. Dog picks up ball, deposits it on her two brown sandals. Another throw. "We are thrown" into what were causes and effects.

The Russians are pulling back, or the Russians are simply regrouping. Their supplies are exhausted, or the heroic Ukrainian army pushes them back. You are given two choices for every instant of the narrative, and neither one ends the war. From above, Mariupol appears completely destroyed. That's the only angle we're given in this news cycle. Trump calls for Putin to help him destroy Biden. Again. A canary's outcry buried in a coal mine.

In the city of fact, there we feel free, or at least stable, even when the earth occasionally shakes, or the ocean trembles afterward. The defender has the advantage in street fighting, and a ruined building's as good as a new one, when your role is to sit in the crotch of a window frame and fire your weapon onto the street. Can you imagine, many soldiers don't even consult their scopes? They fire wildly at buildings, because buildings signify human beings, each framed by a blank window. If glass is transparency, then broken glass is not.

The empty window frame is also a screen. The photograph, however contrived, doesn't lie. We are our own ghosts on this walk; one photograph stuns time, while the other lets it go. Time, the not-image of a woman walking down a street in the bombed out city. Three weeks ago the sun shone on a public square and people walked slowly through their lives' still frames. A man runs with his suitcase toward a train, heading west. Inside the still coherent window, a girl smiles at him. End of photograph.

Genre Issues in War-Time

31 March 2022

Screen of ‘apapane song: are we talking depth or surface? The bulldozer’s a lousy tuba. Flat screen offers false depth. The depth I hear is only surface because it fades like a slow shutter speed in bright light. We sense the leg without seeing it. Its surface is mist, not sturdy enough to walk on, though she’s lighting across campus on her “good” leg. More students are ghosts now. One teacher talked for 50 minutes to a student who rose only sometimes above speech’s threshold. The portal caught, like a tube filling with lava. No one to surf the molten rock; no one to mold word bits into word shapes.

Humanitarian convoy stopped by Russian troops outside of Mariupol. The only way to survive is to leave and to leave is to lose your (sense of) place. Death as surplus loss, inflation of shattered things. One side kills civilians, the other POWs. We call both unethical. A new orchid fell in the rain last night and broke near the top. Don’t worry, it’ll bloom again in another year, Bryant said.

Idealism as the mist that sticks around for a while after its own destruction. To accept its loss as wisdom, embracing halves like rust's accidental bounty. All of it accidental. She keeps working to keep the war at bay. I am given contemplation to catch her words like small birds. When I went into the kitchen this morning, a small brown bird looked in, then flickered away in early light. ʻŌmaʻo?

Above all, do not disturb us. And do not disturb us when we're being entertained. Will Smith's slap resounds more loudly than missile strikes in Kyiv. It shocks us to our bones, that someone would mix genres in that way. It's the death of form by another form, imported from film.

But back to idealism. It's a fixture like a faucet or a drain, witnessing water's creases and songs. The faucet envies water its reality principle, one that remains only in its coming and going. That paragraph doesn't flow, a student might say, without knowing what words open, and which shut down. There's nothing the faucet can do with the nature of water. A spider knows to make its web from faucet to handle, not from faucet to drain.

"We need a new paradigm." Need a world without politicians or leaders or followers or weapons or those who grow rich on their use (which is mandated to avoid warehousing your profits). To die would be one such shift, to turn one's face away. But barring that, you look out your window at the small brown bird looking in, catch your breath at an enormous web woven between tropical leaves. Even the bulldozer has its place in this lessening. You can't invent a ritual to make it all go away, but you can imagine inventing one. Project that on your window screen; brown hapu`u monk bows.

A Note from the Meek

3 April 2022

Contemplation and power connect, like freeway spaghetti, fly-overs whose destination you can only guess, though you keep your foot on the pedal. When you get to the other side, you're still lost, but at least not racing through air like a lost pilot. I have time this morning to look at photographs of the dead in Bucha. Men in drab brown pants, hands tied behind their backs, lying on hard concrete. Dead women in trenches. (Flashback to previous massacre.) A man in a well, sunken. Death isn't sleep, because damaged objects don't rest. They're scattered as trash in a now liberated city, amid the grinning skulls of apartment buildings. Dwell on that.

Take an inventory of your responses. None of them has currency; they're as starved as the ruble. Feelings trapped in a container, the air going out of it. Perverse squash court of anger, disgust, nausea. None of it a whit of good to them. Say your mantras, John told me; they work. I can't push them hard enough to get them to Kyiv. And pushing is the wrong tack.

Nine people shot in Sacramento, more in Texas. Tomorrow the day MLK was shot dead on the balcony of a motel. Lorraine. I remember the name, and that of his assassin. What's memory for? It's an iteration that involves me. I hold to it, try to let it go, fail, then assume the burden of simply watching. In the sitcom, Zelenskyy regards a watch Putin wears and turns his back on it.

The rose is no more beautiful than the rust on an old container in a field. We can cut a rose, but not a band of rust. We can buy a canvas, but not sheet metal anchored to earth. We can see the rust, the rose, the dead bodies in the street, their geometries turned this way and that, face down, bodies bent as if posed. Neither my anger nor my grief reaches that street, though it may touch my screen. The screen is a way in, but also a walling out. One poet cites another poet on yet another poet and we're reassured by the echoes. We think of them as wisdom.

Dear Y, who tweets from Ukraine. Your window view turns white with snow. Your voice alludes to massacres. Your tweets have made a community of the meek. We'd better inherit this earth.

Free Printable Coupons

5 April 2022

Take this free pass to murder. Leave a dotted line of bodies on the road through Bucha. Leave trenches full of bodies you don't cover. Leave chalk white hands tied behind the backs of the dead. Leave a closed hand, nails red with polish and blood. Exchange your coupon for a slashed throat, a cut-off leg, a raped woman trashed by the road. Leave.

"They kill us for their sport." Take this coupon for a dead hen, a toy for your son, an appliance for your wife, then load them on your armored personnel carrier. Don't worry about intercepts; they already know what you're doing.

A boy died in a basement because he caught pneumonia. An old woman shows a reporter how to get down her ladder into the the dark hold of her house. What they can't see they can still bomb, because bombs have such good eyes.

Desire to release the day's news, to internalize my feelings in objects I see go by, as in a Chagall painting, flying like a dog in air in a bathroom on a wall. To take the bells and put them inside my chest, to pull their ropes and fill the cave with a sound at once hollow and dense. To make myself a bell and toll for every nerve ending's complaint. After you complain, you become The Complainer. After you take a photograph of the homeless man bent beneath his pack, he becomes The Pilgrim. What is real doesn't stay that way, or at least what looks real. On Kapahulu this evening, they push their shopping carts toward the sea. In the morning, they retreat up the avenue, while at night they surge back toward Waikiki. They keep our time. Next to Zippy's, a man lies partly shaded by a large umbrella leaning on the ground; he lies on a towel, reading a book.

The war's a metronome, like dementia. It clicks away in the corner to the tune of my keyboard, accreting words, if not their meanings. From a drone's eye view, much of Bucha's completely destroyed, except for the central cathedral. In Cambodia, the poorest villages have gold-leafed temples. Vestigial worship.

An engine starts outside my townhouse. The contemplative life of a machine is noisy and stinky. Many days, I suspect mine is too. How do I act as witness to suffering I feel only as reflected light? My whole life has been an appropriation. My skin is a sieve, and in that sluice I find pieces of us. A poet, wrote Borges, is a person who believes her metaphors are true.

Format and Texture

8 April 2022

The way the word "form" surrenders to "format." The format of my thoughts has no curves or textures beyond this flat screen. Everything that matters lives off-screen, the ginger cat casting her yellow eyes out from the brown railing, the other cat crying, the third cat seated on his favorite chair. For these are our stations. Over 50 dead at a train station in the Ukraine. The "after" photograph shows no human beings, just their bags. Insouciant objects, pink flashing the absent presence of a girl child.

"Believe only what you see" cedes to "believe only what you believe." The loss of old theories leads us to tabloid conspiracies, lacking candles or altars or wine. I wrote about suffering; she referred to my Incandescent Whiteness. Witness. She offers her ass to Nice White Women. I'll kiss my own, thanks.

Palm sounds are not percussion, not yet melody. The myna's song lacks melody, but is not siren. Low rumble of traffic an indistinguishable bass line. It's the microphone that makes them cohere, or a pre-chant of the ear.

The museum creates a form, or is it format?

What shall we put in this museum of our feelings? The love one feels at night when one or the other cat nuzzles; the elation at poems that are more comrades than words; early morning texts about the weather? If the weather is a problem, I suggested, take your photographs *of* the weather.

The university email reported an "incident" and was signed "Student Housing." It urged students to take care of themselves and each other. Student Housing wrote with a heavy heart. Student Housing is there to talk. Student Housing cannot say what the incident was, though someone died. Student Housing refers students to Student Counseling, which is to be distinguished at this institution from Student Health. Student Housing has reached out. Student Housing has an office in the dorm where the student died. Into Student Housing we pour our hopes and fears. God save Student Housing.

There is so much to see beyond this patch of pixels, this white space inside a gray space, framed by black. When asked what gets in the way of my spiritual practice, I said "memory." It's a peculiar neurosis, this need to put memories in containers and place them on the belt like sushi. Others talk about planning, making lists, worrying about the day's tasks. I worry that memory is my task.

The leaf blower starts up; one cat comes forward, then walks past; I'm stationed on the floor. My back hurts. In response to the world, we hurt ourselves. There must be a word for that.

Redemption Song

9 April 2022

The disharmony of our conversations. There's no more monotone, only clutches of mixed notes. We still want to learn about each other's desires, about the histories that might make sense of all this, but we're folded in like a t-shirt whose imprinted face more resembles an alien than Bob Marley. Or that speaks of the miracle of walking on the earth and that there is an elf. Never quote Oppen on a shirt; lose one letter and it's all over, the clear bell of meaning ceding to demented sentences saved to our clouds.

I said I wished I hadn't talked so much. She assured me it was a conversation; there were two of us, ears pressed to phones, and there were two voices gathering up work and suicide, homesickness and grief. It was as if the earth took Marthe after she'd gone and the Kapoho tidepools filled with molten lava. Reclamation project by one angry woman of another. When I took black rocks for her husband from the beach, I told Pele what I was doing. But that was not a conversation. Prayer leaves the interlocutor out.

One Y took a photograph from the Kyiv to Warsaw train. The land is flat and white, a bit blurred by the train's speed. The subject appears anonymous, if land could be without a name. When we doubt our memory, we take up our machines to capture it. Put them in the folders, the albums, all the dead metaphors that litter our screens. Some day we'll be reminded by iPhoto that we have memories they cherish for us.

The suicide squeeze failed last night. You only succeed if you survive to score a run. The young woman who succeeded will be doubly forgotten. There were cops and firefighters and a memorial that quickly disappeared. Since we cannot say our grief, let's stand to hear the sirens, the alarm bells, the leaf blowers and weed whackers, all the instruments of our grieving.

My husband calls me on Facetime from the Mauna Loa road. After days of rain, the sky is a clear blue. He pans the scene down the mountain: the road's yellow zipper, the koa trees. He is happy, the dog is happy, and I will say that I am, too.

Committee Work

11 April 2022

Memory as dream work, if it's work at all. Tell me how to modulate my voice out of this anger, another death on campus, forgotten in advance "because of privacy issues." Privacy's a form of active forgetting, as if by not attaching a name to death, it had not happened, at least not in that way. The approved ways include heart attack and car accident. We have not yet gathered as a committee to discuss the feasibility of approving suicide, whether it is committed or merely completed. To define success in this instance would be to mandate a cloak be placed over the frail bosom of information. It's not an act against God but against information, so it's suppressed.

The difference between bathos and tragedy, my friend suggests, might lie between self-pity and a dialogue that leads to it. If I give my dog a voice in this sequence, she will have none in editing it. So I leave her to her silences, her barks of greeting, warning, and pleas for help when tangled up on her long leash. What I can't translate I might still write down. A writer divorced from her translator cannot read herself. Type in your sentence about a blocked pipe and get back the word "evacuation" in French. Those who can't evacuate do not become refugees. They may lie in the rubble of Mariupol. They're fighting to hold a city that no longer exists.

They'll drop just enough chemical weapons to push at the boundaries of military protocol. If war is a game, then one side is bombing the board, destroying its plastic houses and hotels, passing go without taking money, then writing "for the children" on their bombs.

If the bombers write that, does that make them the dark parents of those children, aiming their metal sperm-shaped ordinance at a train station, one that gives and receives cars full of human beings? No one is fleeing now. If you stay you're likely to die, but if you leave you're likely to die, so why not stay in the ruins of the city you remember from your childhood?

I am far away from Mariupol, but so are those who write from Kyiv.

Maeve head butts me, snuggles with me at night, then attacks Claude with ruthlessness. He sits on the old red chair, stained, sagging, and licks at his wounds. The cats have their own wars and peaces. Warning: graphic images. Please do not show that image of abuse ever again.

"Whatchu doing taking pictchas of my fucking house? Erase that shit from your phone," a young man hisses at me in Kalihi. I don't put up the photo of his house, with the ad beside it for Dyke's Market, which takes EBT and says so on a sign covered with images of beer cans. He follows me up the street, but I turn away from him and walk. The next photos are of Bob Marley, a walk-up apartment with a tiny American flag flying on a stick.

Flag Ships (of our disposition)

15 April 2022

So that's what flagship means, a child might say to the curmudgeon watching the news: the commanding officer carries the flag on the lead ship. Not to be confused, in this instance, with leadership. A cartoon shows mermaids underwater beside a gun turret, marveling at how they always wanted to see Moscow. Ship stands in for, sinks for the place, which stands in for the nation, sinking. In the line-up of rhetorical tropes, only one commits the crime.

So that's what a flagship is, a metaphor on top of a symbol on top of a military reference. The provost of our flagship university writes to a woman who told him about her mother's suicide, "there is simply no truth to this." After the vice chancellor, on reading my email about a suicide on campus responded, "Enjoy your retirement!" a friend noted that the exclamation point was shrapnel.

One cat attacks another cat. Second cat taken to vet, where he bites a tech. Vet tech taken to the hospital. Second cat sits on the left side of the lanai. First cat moves from right to left side, stares, her tail wiggling. Words wouldn't end this hostility; they never do. "Should we take Putin seriously when he warns of unpredictable actions?" No, says the pundit.

Age creates a gap between cause and effect. Get your certificate in self-detection. Trace back the symptom (wrenched back) to cause (pulling morning glory vines) as if to freshly discover a link. The pundit knows better. It's a proxy war, ginned up by NATO. There is always someone at the controls, even when the ship sinks. It's genocide, if that word means anything. It's a series of war crimes. It's something we can name, because naming it marks it like a flag. Unmarked graves are lines on a map, as are the convoys of trucks through a forest. Lines used to make sense.

The historian geometer gets out her ruler and traces patterns. Lines become angles become triangles become shattered squares. Lines cross the map like a Trail of Tears; one of them is the Trail of Tears. *Ain't no real big secret all the same.*

Y's new photo looks out from the middle of a giant skyscraper on other looming apartment blocks. The new photo is as banal as the old, just taken from higher up. She's back in Kyiv, inviting us to share her #warcoffee. The offending cat has come in from the deck to eat the other cat's food. The other cat sits beneath a railing, out of sight. What he can't see won't hurt him.

A friend lashes out about platitudes. Life is suffering, he says, and no prayer to end it will ever succeed. He's suffering, and that becomes his title, because titles comfort us. Another friend reminds me that a dog talks in *Anna Karenina*. A third friend doesn't name his dog Tolstoy. My screen fills with other peoples' flowers, cherry blossoms mostly. Gratitude is one of these platitudes, but like any, it's harder to breathe in than to spit it out.

—for Patrick Pritchett

What I Thought Was Short Cut Proved to be Bog

16 April 2022

What I'd thought was a short-cut proved to be a bog. Sunken nearly to my knees, I looked to my right and saw the large pipe, the bridge, evidence of an occasional stream. My sandals sit by the door, hosed down, still smelling of Hau`ula peat. I walked barefoot—except for the mud—to one of three memorials on the beach: three for two men. A name in the tree, "Ku." A banner, flags. More likely, there are three for one man, Braddah Ku, shown twice, younger and older, on one banner. I find him on-line. He was 48.

At another beach park I find a tree decorated with water floats; underneath is a red chair, looking out to sea. In the tree's crook, faded photos of a woman and a boy. Under the tree, on the ocean side, sit empty wine bottles and a small pair of red tennis shoes. This was not a drowning but a car crash.

Bryant says his friend is depressed; they talk nearly every day now. His daughter leaves for college soon, and his parents are old, a thousand miles away. Last night they talked about tanks getting killed in the Ukraine. How when a tank gets hit, it's repaired. A crew goes in to clean out the dead's pieces, to make the tank seem new, except there are always stains in the cracks. Like hotel staff, they clear the armored room for another set of occupants, precarious in their hutches. Everyone knows it. "When I died, they washed me out of the turret with a hose." I send the link. For god's sake, talk next about flowers.

The need to know, to understand these waves of political and military history, set against the need to stay above water, to not drown. To make memorials inside of our conversations, as we look at the white-topped waves of a large blue ocean. To confront the axis of linear and circular time, without leaping into its saw. See saw see saw. Saw sea.

On-line, I find a photograph of the car's wreckage, a story about the mother and her son and two visitors from Utah who survived their end of the accident. I find a photograph of the young woman who died at Crouching Lion, a video of her grieving friend. My research is remembrance, made whole-cloth of others' words and pictures, a memorial of memorials. What good does this do to me or to anyone? Not evidence of war crimes, or memories cherished for the families; not altars made to poetry, or even prose. Could I not simply drive past?

I drove back home, feet and trousers black with mud, sandals in the trunk of the car. The trip smelled of mud. In the photograph, my foot appears sculpted, toe nails outlined in mud, the bluish straps mere suggestions. It's the smell of earth, of death becoming life, of sweet water so close to the salt ocean. "Is that Hawaiian mud?" a cousin asks. The ʻāina, rich with stink, my toenails still black with it. Clean and unclean memory. The flowers, the ones that had not faded, were bright. For "Papa," a red lei and yellow sunflowers, hanging from a palm.

Garden Rocket

20 April 2022

A green rocket grows in the man's garden. Rooted by its nose, fin blossoms stretch out from a metal stalk. Earth parts with few traces of violence. He's alive, he says, though he was beaten. Another rocket bears its awful fruit elsewhere.

These are its stages: train platform, littered with bags; vacant-eyed buildings, empty; littered streets; forest encampment cluttered with cans. Or, the steel mill in Mariupol, resting on tunnel roots. Suck the tunnel walls of their water. Learn from rats how to abide the dark.

Lilith and I meet a woman named Noni. I ask if she's the same Noni whose name I saw earlier on a missing dog sign. Fifi's been found. Fifi was struck by lightning, dug a tunnel to get her pups out, refused to emerge from under the water tank after Noni took her in. Fifi is unfriendly. "We're all getting rickety," she says. "I look in the mirror and wonder what happened. I still feel the same." Stranger still the photograph of ther as a young woman, though neither she nor I say so.

Beauty takes time, the philosopher opines, while information does not. The powers that be are in it to destroy time, consign us to the quirky eternity of work. Even your breaks are part of seamless days of data collection. A mirror's side-eye captures a warped image of my dog beside a dirt driveway. Ferns held up by old propane tanks, their buds rusted, numbers blurring. We don't have time, because time has no edges, just wrinkles where the fins wagged.

"Are you still obsessed with time?" my mother asked me then.

It's the smoothness he distrusts: smoothness of metal dogs, smoothness of "good" skin, smoothness of elevator music. We don't remember what isn't interrupted. Memory's born of hiccup. In memory, there is an other, and she is we. The girl who ignored her parents is now the parent who tries to catch the eye of her girl. Forgiveness is salve for regret.

One student didn't want to see the faces of the dead on photos of road memorials. Not symbolic enough. Memories depend on rust. Only a clean surface gets forgotten, and where is the symbol there? A young woman stares out from a frame, ribbon lei on both sides. She is smiling; her body is full. A sign warns us to go no farther.

“You’re taking photos of the memorials, but not what happens to them.”

The Fake Flowers of Highway 11

24 April 2022

Do I shoot wide or narrow? Take in the filthy stuffed bear and the slightly cleaner pink pig? Linger on crosses supported by rusted bed frames, wheels dangling? Take a portrait of the portrait of the man named below, beside the cross that bears his dates, camouflaged by flowers? Cross the highway to see the memorial from a dispassionate distance? Aim my camera at the cars that streak by? Make sure they blur? Look for the passengers looking at me, but not the gloves, the stethoscope, the smudged notes? Notice the not-noticing by taking pictures of it. One memorial consisted of artificial flowers—appropriate to the tropics—rimmed with dirt from mowers and car spray. Nowhere was there a name, a bear, a note; the memorial was itself unidentified. What feeling do you get from the memorial stripped of any recollection?

A Ukrainian woman on twitter posts the photograph of a young blonde woman. Putin's gift, Zelenskyy calls it, her death by bomb on Easter weekend, along with her baby, shown with mother, with bottle. We think: good for propaganda. We regret that thought. There's no dispassion in my looking at her, only in counting the dead on a street I've never walked. But numbers, too, bleed. Leave all the feeling to the audience, the teacher says, but I require content. Or consent.

From the road you can't see that the firefighter was Jon Hara, that he liked to fish, that he used a stethoscope, that his teeshirt had his name on it. I took the wrinkled t-shirt photo, still in my phone, and thought of Marie Hara, her husband Jon. When I turned on instagram, the first photograph was of Marie's daughter. The second was of Jon.

What the Hoarders Left Behind

29 April 2022

Old joy stick, wreathed in webs. Two pink elephants, laughing in theirs. Premium oil, Value Power car battery. Old rubber ball, once red, now flecked, beside the yellow tool. Old string of white Christmas lights on the chain link fence. On the porch, a crumpled up American flag to go with a sticker on the moldy truck window. Stacks of flat cardboard, boxes of old spray cans, cleaners, squirt bottles. No one's been here for weeks. This is not quite narrative, not quite not narrative. Diary of objects, the dirty carport its frame. Hard to decide which photo to take, which to leave.

She puts a photograph of herself and her mother in her war diary. They are ordinary, but so is the war. I can't write a proper one, as I don't look at TikTok or read the articles about rape as a military strategy. After you listen to a trauma story, you double up, breathe in, fold back into seated position. Later, you drive down Haunani, where an old woman trudges, looking lost, carrying her Target bag.

You don't stop to ask if she needs a ride. Your ticket got punched this morning.

She was her father's "experiment," left in a room alone to see how she reacted. My friend says there was no kindness in her house growing up. She found kindness in her 50s. Avoidance of story was my self-care.

So many of the abandoned objects have to do with cleaning, lubing, fixing, making stuff work. Yellow oil bottles sit like trophies on the carport frame. The only vehicle is pinned in place by junk, by mold, by disuse. I love the old trucks whose beds have ginger growing in them.

Mass graves left by the hoarders of war. Loss is accumulation. We have more than you, so we lose. You have more than we do, so you lose. The man down the street screamed obscenities when he played video games. His dead joy stick half smashed in the carport. Easier to name the joy stick than the flowers across the road, purple prods melting in the rain.

Heidegger as a Cure for Anxiety

2 May 2022

"Anxiety could be experienced as a kind of calm by holding yourself out, into that experience": moments when you're past worry, adrenaline-surfing, full of everything you can't name except it moves quickly, curling like a leaf around itself on asphalt, mottled brown and darker brown, and I wondered why friends thought about colors in poetry, as it was the thoughts that seemed most to count, and count they did, by 25s or 100s, in math that was not yet critical race theory, or anything except raw numbers. The four on a telephone pole sits upside down, making the shape of an "I" with a handle, as if we could hold our first person up to our lips and drink. If we take "calm" to mean stillness, not a steady being in yourself, then calm it is. Renovate your words and they will mean what you need them to mean.

Dissolving vignettes, each a single take, holding itself out until stopping in mid-air, which is mid-time, which is the space of an absent narrative, or at least of one that cannot find its ending. What we think is true—a woman captured by a psychopath in a metal container—ends. When next we see her, she's ironing. The psychopath wants her to show her "true face," not the one she assumes. The torturer always looks for truth, because the means justify whatever ends. Body, story, the tweets of Russian torture victims you can't see because they're "disturbing." Scroll past to see the latest trades, the low batting averages, the poetry gossip. That tweet is a trap-door, but you leap over it the way your dog does a puddle when a car comes. The water breaks into shadow pieces; her tongue sticks out, offering a hint of color in the drab overcast light.

Those still trapped in Mariupol's steel factory have moved past anxiety, because where they exist is true. Anxiety assumes, but when it's proven, it dissolves into an after-calm, horrifying and yet certain. This is not how you imagine relieving your anxiety; mostly, you think of yourself lying comfortably on a beach, once again able to breathe in, out. But the steel mill is the labyrinth that promises to hide you long enough to become accustomed. To hunger, to terror, to fingers that push on walls, but cannot feel them. Hongly described his body as it starved, his arms eating themselves. New Yorkers, we read, are now terrified.

We haven't lost our sense of proportion, though that is our ambition. It's our stage, where the player in a slump gets sent to Mariupol and the soldier in the tank gets to attend his own bobble head day at the park. Four men in a tank dream of meadows full of flowers. The tank dreams of its origins apart from war. And the war dreams it's trapped inside a music room without a key. I'll turn the house inside out to look for it. In the meantime, lock it all out as she did the mean lover who shot faces on the subway. Piles of books lie on the curb, each bearing the title, ETHICS.

Note: quote by Simon Critchley, in "A Philosopher Laughs at Death..." by Mark Dery. *The Chronicle of Higher Education*, April 28, 2022. Thanks to Jon Morse, who sent me the link. Some details come from *Code Unknown*, a film by Michael Haneke.

Suburb or Refuge

5 May 2022

Keeping score doesn't matter if you lose. Not the next election, but the last. Scorecards hold history inside of repetition; each score staged within a diamond inscribed in grass. I use memory to visualize shapes and colors; the generator's missing, but not the videotape. Memory's a form of kompromat. Regret enables forgiveness, mandates regret, as a player runs the bases, tripping around third, caught in the bog of rules and an unforgiving baseline. Bryant follows the tally of dead tanks, dead transport vehicles, dead Russians. I watch video of a children's park destroyed by artillery shells. There goes the red slide, and there the plastic fortress wall. Open it up; there are no people.

The photograph draws you out into the drop of rain on a green stem beside curled brown ferns. The photo doesn't live outside history but so far inside it you might drown. Earlier years were about thinking about being, parsing it, making metaphors of it, as if-fing it until the thread wound around your brain like the dog's leash around fern trunks. Appropriate for the suburbs, when details appear to be claimed by the city, and your house promises refuge from them. "But this was meant to be our refuge," a woman said of her new house, after thefts were reported. The suburbs are anti-photographic. Leave this note on your door: "Gone to seek refuge." *Revel in your abandon.*

Photograph of a Ukrainian journalist, killed in action. To see him is to know him gone. His image is his obit. What is in front of us is absent from us. Is this how symbolism starts? Does it matter? Symbol as payback for our losses, money as a kind of poetry. The spreadsheet is a comfort form, like a score card or the metal grid at the front of a tractor. There's a bent square the spider chose for her web, but the rest is relentless same. In order to straighten the image, you place it inside a grid and turn slowly until it slips into place. She asked why my verticals were not vertical. When I went back to look, the rusted poles were bent. The photograph's fidelity was to its leaning.

Raindrops. They cling to stems, sit on petals, fall from angel trumpets. I watch the iPhone's screen try to arrive at clarity. When it does, I push the button. Otherwise, I move on. Focus is as random as the drop itself. Go with the chaos, a student says, or organize it in a frame.

Dear Mr. Buddha

10 May 2022

The recommended books of the day include *Grief*, *Shame*, *Anger*, and other vestments of our time. Our strategies for coping are old, and we need primers on how to act, or not. Fear is mother of them all. My quarrel is with the prepositions. For, at. The lens set too far back for in or with. I'm astounded at; I'm sorry for; I'm stricken by. But rain it keeps raining on the broad leaves and the narrow, the fuschia with their funny hats, angel trumpets with their fuzzy stems. No need for prepositions if you get close enough. Except in.

The big words are short, saxon. But the weak are pusillanimous, preoccupied with syllables instead of sound. Meaning's the remainder you get when you divide anything with everything. You have a plastic shed outside in which to store it, but space is getting crowded, musty, and meanings congeal, glued together by proximity. I went out looking for one, but couldn't remember which, whether it was dry or cooked, smoked or rotten. Hoping to connect meaning with its provocation, I measured my feelings: half-part anger, half-part shame, with full-on apathy as my shield. But when the object denoting joy got confused with the one denoting grief, I entered the territory of mixed feelings. Time is said to un-mix them, by stirring and then leaving to settle like river silt. But where's the time these days?

The steel mill is held by fascists and attacked by other fascists. Their languages are proximate, if not identical, as are their weapons. The names they call each other matter less than their flags, which don't call but represent. They do not yell at, but merge with, the colors blue and yellow, darker blue and red. I really miss the Soviet anthem, don't you? Their trance is war. We manufacture it with the big words, then melt it down into syllabits. Let memory be for a blessing, or let it not be.

We cloak our likes inside of hearts, a misfit anatomy. To like is either to notice, to appreciate, to curry favor, but we can't find the context with our arrows. Write slogans to self about not-knowing, then know when to apply them. A fundamentalism of ambiguity seems preferable to one of certitude, though the most certain bail out when questioned. The air is full of parachutes. We return to earth chastened, without claim, but need propels us toward the simple sentence. An eye in the ground from which a red-leaved vine travels. Its stare is fixed and so, we fear, are we.

A Mirrored Stage

13 May 2022

Watch only the beginning of each video. See Russian soldiers open a glass door, but turn them off. See policemen approach a Black man on the street; turn them off. It's not to create suspense; suspense consists in looking back. Where did this begin, and how do we know when to click the button off? Like McCartney inventing "Get Back," but lacking the final concert on the roof. There were cops there, too, who ended it early. Go backwards from there, like a song that tells you which band member is dead (hint: he's one of those still alive). There's pleasure in going back to a song's origins, but not in returning to the scene of a war crime starting to unfold. The inverse of narrative is a cliff.

Atrocity is forced narrative. It stops time where time wasn't meant to be stopped, kills it with as much certainty as the journalist shot in the head by a soldier. To create peace, give time back to story, allow it to unfold as slowly as a green bud with purple highlights, denoting the color it will become without a megaphone announcement. Or dissolve it all together, refusing to show the opening of the door, the soldiers entering, cops exiting. I prefer my photographs still on Instagram, precisely because they go nowhere. Stories are all addition; I lay out my coins like a child at the cash register. "You should really learn how to do this yourself," one clerk said to me at five or six.

An enormous white cloud drifts across the window to the right; in front, an absolute gray. The collision will occur where the blind spot in my townhouse lies, at an angle just past the television, the speakers, all our forms of output. Absolute is only approximate, but it's dense. A cat sniffs the deck, laps up some dirty water. A red plastic pot lies on its side on a tan plastic chair, divided into shadow and light. No, I don't write poems about my photographs. The relationship is more intimate, less about "about," more a parallel construction.

Topical is timely, also an ointment. Tropical is moist and warm, also figurative. *J'essuie donc je suis*, I said, but everyone thought I'd made a mistake. If mother is a job, as Bryant said, so are we. Not acting, quite, but something akin.

The teacher said his favorite student's image was inside a box. Each student came to peer in. Surprise, awkwardness, laughter. What was inside the box, but mirror, light moving so fast no child could tell her own face from the one that peered back at her. Glass bottom boats are like ancestry.com. We see us as we truly were.

At Kualoa Beach Park

26 May 2022

After Columbine. After Red Lake. After West Nickel Mines Amish School. After Virginia Tech. After Northern Illinois University. After Oikos. After Sandy Hook. After UC Santa Barbara. After Umqua Community College. After Marjorie Stoneman Douglas High School. After Santa Fe High School. After Robb Elementary School. After.

A monk seal slept at the water's edge, her scarred gray belly looming in the air, head only barely twitching when the water reached it. (We agreed that was a good sign.) A small flipper tucked under her large gray body. Three men had driven close in vans; their job was to make a barricade between us and the seal. Do not get within 100 feet. On our way out, I told a tourist about the monk seal; "what's that, honey?" her friend said.

What does the word "after" mean? Can it live without "before," or is it "before"? After, but ahead of the next event. After, on the altar of human sacrifice. Parents could not recognize their children, had to provide DNA. (And what if they were adopted?) The horrible dementia of violence, that it takes away our memory because it redacts faces, blows limbs apart, drenches clothes in blood. Memory comes back as repetition ("repetition is one of my triggers," she said) as the awful moment before you forget everything. Again. It leaves a space for the classroom's return as the place in your head you can never get out of. The doors are locked, except one the gunman walked through. Senator Cruz blames the door. Governor Abbott the mentally ill. They speak of evil. The man who confronts them is uncivil. Because who would dare speak of such a thing when it just occurred? Before we speak, we must be after. But after is now dead.

Lilith and I walk up hill. Two little girls take turns posing in front of a small palm, the taller girl wearing a long black and white dress. First one and then the other smiles. Their young mother takes pictures. They are so beautiful—and ("and" is addition, I say to my students, not conjunction) they could be killed by a boy/man not much older than they are. It could happen after they hold up their honor student certificates. It could happen after lunch. It could happen after, or before. Last day of school? I ask. I take their picture, and hand the phone back. Streams of children flow toward the elementary school. We know the tide has an edge you dare not cross. So we trace its curve along the sand, leaning over to pick up shells, fish skeleton, blue plastic bottle with frayed hieroglyphics scrawled at its base. Spry cordage.

Impermanence ought not be slaughter.

—*for Ruth Canham*

The Poetry of Quietude

28 May 2022

"We were good. We were good. We stayed quiet." Even the child hit on the nose by a bullet remained quiet, as did the teacher, bleeding from her leg. The ones who could be seen played dead; the others prayed. What makes them prey, these innocents? He wanted to be close to them, his mother said. When one girl said "help," he shot her. The intimacy of bullets. I could not bear the thought of intimacy until the wound closed, a bit. Rape by bullet a false intimacy, sick in its equation of blood not with relation but with its breaking.

A second cat comes to sniff the chair on which a third cat had slept. She is utterly quiet, even as her nose moves. I sit on the floor typing, while the dog sleeps. Our silence is under threat from birds, from traffic, from the man coughing upstairs. Which way do you run, when the shooting starts?

"I don't want any more moments of silence," he says. Can there not be outrage in such quiet, between the storms?

We know the next one comes, because murder is a weather pattern, and patterns repeat. Hope wind turns the other way so you can breathe, then worry when it stops. When our memories melt like sand, make glass. To see brings us close. To see through keeps us quiet. Someone look inside the windows of that classroom and take it all back.

The war diary has moved home. If you can count to ten, you can breathe for them. If you breathe for them, won't they come home again?

Where the palm was cut, I found the image of an outer space creature, wings flung out from its orange face, a yellow collar composing the image for me. If you look close enough, nothing pretends to make sense.

At the Tomb of the Known Quantity

30 May 2022

Today's "current events" will be as obscure as a dial phone by next year, but I wrap myself inside them like a hair shirt on a baroque composer, who thinks his fugue will cure memory of its scabs. We forgot all the old people shopping in Buffalo when the kids were killed in Uvalde. Our senses of place make none. Names as headstones, just as apt to fail. Take photos of the spalling to mark the disintegration of concrete as it falls away from rebar. Everything is a mark: this word, that photo, old conflicts butting into the repeat sign. We won't give Ukraine rockets that reach Russia, the president says. A domesticated war, though the word "genocide" pops up like a question, or a popsicle, melting into our inability to define terms. Term limits might help, but they're just other borders snapping shut.

Wish me a "Happy Memorial Day" and I'll tell you some memories are worth misplacing. We praise memory for keeping our losses alive, families under umbrellas at the cemetery this morning, children fanning out to play, little girl with hula hoop. She said she was bored of memory, but it's my perpetual borer, worm weaving the silk screen of my brain, a wooden frame to hold cloth still. Dying for, so honored. Dying as, forgotten. One little girl who danced wanted a Tiktok account. Her parents told her she was too young. In her murdered absence, they create it themselves.

At the cemetery, the men call me Aunty and scratch Lilith's head, her flanks, call her a good dog. Today, the place crawls with local folks, including two old women bearing stacks of ginger. Tomorrow, it's back to tourist buses, to phones thrust from car windows to shoot the mountains. To drive through is not to be, though to be is rather like a drive through. Always the clouds of impermanence. We can't grieve because there are no intervals. So we check out of Hotel Mourning to watch an action film. He said when his father-in-law died, he watched three action movies in one evening. He didn't feel good when he woke up.

You Take the Window Seat

31 May 2022

Before we were disposable, we had friends. Before our hearts turned to plastic, we made them into metaphors. Before I began to write this, I thought I'd venture into happiness. Where you are my harbor, the crook of your arm my consolation. Where, when I lie on you, your body calms itself from trembling. Give in to move on. The small words are all signs, in a relative sense, pointing to something more than relative, though less than enlightened, perhaps. When W.G. Sebald ran into Tom Hardy at an intersection, they spoke of coincidence (there is none) and of experience as a map, spooling like tape to touch a ruler, erect, that measures vertical space. To react too strongly to a map is a sign of trauma, because the map itself can't bear witness. It's just a throw rug on which we either walk or fall down. Slippery slopes are often real, even when they're flat. His flag (in space) so close to my childhood (in time) that memory starts its demented walk down a long hallway, slow and stiff.

Before we had friends, we were disposable. A blue toy,

lacking hands and feet, left by the mower and his retinue of egrets. The mother Mary, whose fingers were chipped, now stands without her hands—stacked below her on the ground. The next day, one hand lies in the road, smashed.

I take a photograph of an old black pick-up truck; in the back are an old broom, leaning against the back window, door just ajar, and a purple net at the end of a pole. I try to get both broom and pole in the photograph, or broom and window, but nothing works. A man yells at me from down the parking lot. "Whatchu taking picchas of?" I tell him the broom. I say no harm. He yells "ass" at me. Mine, or his, I don't know. When I look at the photo, I notice his safety sticker is overdue by nearly seven months. Which of us in this moment was not safe?

Her window view is static: her tall apartment building looks out at similar. Time in Kyiv has slowed; she now goes out for coffee, invites her twitter followers in. Chronology's gone in Donbas, each minute laid out on a table to be crushed. There are fingers, but no hands, glass but no windows, the components of wholes without any context. Neither body nor building holds, though eyes and windows stare out. Someone at the coffee shop yelled to put a lid on it.

War and Peace and War Again

3 June 2022

A small pink Skecher for the left foot, illustrated with peace signs and hello kitties, sits on a piece of dull blue wood beside a thick bit of chalk. Hearts and an 888 encircle it. Did a little girl lose the shoe when she lost her life, or did someone bring the shoe, as if in memory of someone that small? So many toys still behind plastic in their boxes, awaiting a child's hand: dolls, a Power Ranger, a small blue and red motorcycle on a stone pedestal. A third grade teacher writes to her former student on a football. He'd liked to throw it. "I'm sorry you went threw this," another note reads.

We watch the borrowed Red Army run naked into a lake. I guess horses were hurt in the making of this film, Bryant says, as they tumble across the screen. Long columns of soldiers march across, but there are no feet hitting earth, or men chanting time. It's a quiet march. As he lies mortally wounded, he keeps seeing one valley in his head. There's nothing to distinguish it from other valleys, except in its repetition for him. A cannon ball spits flame; he thinks he wants to live. We see it in the captions. Film is superficial, but we see into and through it. War's the cruelest edit. The general sits at his chair and eats his lunch. Bodies are draped on trenches, spilling off their little cliffs. The ballrooms of Moscow are not so well tended.

Light is sweet as rock candy. It bathes water drops, at once clarifying and extenuating them. Where I thought there were more drops, I found plastic beads hanging from a gate. I don't mind when beauty makes a fool of me.

Constrain Yourself

4 June 2022

Invent constraints. The dog is one, the phone's lens another. Begin to smile, but don't complete the arc. Make of it a concept divorced from happiness or St. Louis. It must be more difficult than that, like bent trees denoting Alzheimer's. Or dandelions so fragile that they're grand ("this is life," the photographer notes). His is an inverted constraint, concept infecting object with meaning. Does dandelion know it means, or does it simply let the wind take it, like pieces of a mother octopus drifting when she dies? The myth of Dandelion and Octopus has yet to be written, but calls out to be framed as Dispersal.

Comic relief in Tolstoy shares transience with humor, though not its cadence. Alexei, on his back and in pain, sees the clouds and knows them beautiful. Pierre sees an old and a young man shot, a city in flames, a fearful toddler, blood on his shirt, and knows that the human vocation is happiness. He sees Natasha dancing (flashback) and a bloody field (flashback). They merge into a single image, with a single floor. Something needs to change, we say after the latest massacre.

If the word doesn't fit, take another and wrap it around the pole like a snake, its meaning rippling like water, fixed and then unfixed again. Stillness lasts too short a time to merit its name, a "still yet moving bridge" constructed of stone and light, cables and church towers. Leave the citations to me; phrases drift like dancers in the ballroom I live inside of, or it inside of me. If forgetting doesn't work, try forgiveness, which still remembers. If that doesn't work, refer back to the recipe from today's newspaper. You may have neglected to breathe.

Theater of war: theater of dance. Both choreographed, both dissolving at the moment of action. A stopwatch captures an instant when they cross. Take your favorite poem and make of it a dance. You will leap at the sound of a preposition, bow before a noun, stand tall for verbs. Soviet soldiers acted the parts of 19th century Russians. The dogs had to be swapped out, because they didn't want to hunt. A wolf's eyes tracked from side to side, a stick in its mouth. Perhaps it knew earth's beauty at that moment, on the other side of a crowd of men and dogs.

A man yells into his phone on I`iwi Street. “Don’t give me that shit!” Then, as Lilith and I walk by, “it’s such a beautiful day here.”

This Old House

8 June 2022

Happy Death Day dvd box. No inside or outside: the door was open. A kind of reverence fills me when I trespass. Ford a stream of kids' clothes, shoes, toys, boxes where presents were, two small four-wheeled vehicles embraced by vines, spider webs. We enter the living room and get no farther. Past this room a kitchen, from which light streams, then fades. Lilith perches on an old mattress by the front door. She's a bit skittish, too. Outside (truly outside) is the car cemetery, each wreck a museum. On the driver's seat in one, an Oysterizer blender, or at least its base. From the mirror hangs an old air freshener, which reads "leather." Windshield leathery with mildew or moss. The plastic gargoyle that holds a sign "How Much I Love You" had a twin inside the house, beneath a fly's eye chandelier. We're past story, inside of consequence but lacking awareness of cause. A family lived here, and they left. As Lilith and I start back, I spot a child's jacket twisted in a bush, arms akimbo, old zipper undone.

A term like "emptiness" doesn't work. The house is empty of people, but full of what is now called "junk." The clutter inside of emptiness reduces its charm. It's a mind on meditation that swims against a current of plastic gnomes and broken forks, break-ups and break-downs. They put us in our place, then take that place away.

The Words for the Trees

11 June 2022

Recognition scenes are slower now. I know her face, her white hair, her smile. We walk, together with Lilith, until the dog and I reach home. Then I remember the woman who understands the world as it's explained to her by an 18th century French count. She says she didn't know people fed dogs until she left the family farm for college. "People feed dogs!" she'd reported.

Bumpersticker on a new neighbor's truck: something about the 2nd amendment. A large, new American flag hangs outside her small green cottage. The more you connect the dots, the less anyone believes them, because they're dots and not crosses or planets or soccer balls.

Inside the old house I found a calendar from 2016 with weeks in July marked "36th, 37th, 38th." Two stuffed animals hang on one wall, an orange "I Love Daddy" book lies on the floor beside plastic water bottles, an artificial lei, other stuff. On the next wall, family photos: husband

and wife and baby; two young children. An envelope that reads "memories" must have a child's elementary school photos tucked inside. Framed photograph, knocked over, of a baby. Elementary school class photo. One plastic page of an album full of old sports cars. A Phillies towel and a uniform that hangs outside the closet. "Eat the Rainbow," a bag announces. The refrigerator was toxic. On a counter beside it, two dvds of *Hot Jailhouse Babes*. Instagram censors me when I post my photo of them.

A famous actor lives across the street, says gray-haired woman wearing a "Why Be Normal" teeshirt. This used to be a beautiful farm. Someone got sick; someone else took advantage. Our rain forest Pompeii grows cobwebs and dead cars. One senses there are layers to this story, but it's been flattened. We wander inside the end of one plot whose beginning and middle we don't know. Nor do we know what happened next. "Usually, people take their family photos."

Half the residents of this town are seekers, the other half (it sometimes seems) are white men trying to survive themselves. But there are still people to be angry at, those who get TROs out on them. The man who raped an old woman. The man who was thrown out of town, twice. The man who was attacked twice, though in once instance he attacked first. We weren't supposed to know about that first. Watch out for him; he patrols this street, our why-be-normal friend tells us. When they ask what I'm doing, I usually say it's for a photography class.

Dictionaries as Punishments

14 June 2022

Crickets and the horn of a truck moving backwards. Water drop and bird spill. Dog bark, harmonica break. How do you define art?

Mildew etchings on truck windows. Filthy rag tucked beneath windshield wiper. An old blender in the front seat. How do you define technological innovation?

Woman apologizing for her Russian accent. Two years ago, she hated Ukrainians. Another explains Putin to me at Bird Park. How do you define history?

I mix *accordion* with *harmonica*, *hang nail* with *raw hide*. Tip of the tongue syndrome run amok. I cannot say sentences by rote. How do you define language?

My new piece of furniture is a piece of shit. The former AG says his boss spouted bullshit. Lilith's stomach hurt after she ate cat shit. How do you define shit?

Puddles in the road, filled in with gravel. Gravel taken out; she likes to slow the traffic down. Narcissus's face had stones in it. How do you define psychology?

Hilo's homeless line up for food. We drink coffee and tea with healers and tourists. A fake lei hangs from the building across the street. How do you define authenticity?

Neat piles of wires and dry wall the next block over. Red paint on a white board. How do you define context?

Why are old friendships more permanent than newer ones? How do you define the question, *is this true*?

To define is to point. The black pointer, Doxy, doesn't walk so much as weave. What he smells when he points we can't know. How do you define definition?

Patriot Front member, pistol on his teeshirt, yells obscenities at a camera. He sees what we don't, spews syllables at it, threatens it, performs for it. I learn the term "sap glove." How do you define sap?

Do we live with or around the dead? Why do we keep speaking to them, as if they were all ear and we all mouth? In my sleep he heard me say, "I have no further questions."

The Joy Box

16 June 2022

I keep my joy in a terrarium in the corner by the window. Its glass keeps all suffering outside. My shadow digresses between it and what lies outside.

My joy feels itself set apart from the complicated ethics of this moment, testimonies from such a complicated source. Clear water, a sign that warns of lepto from cattle upstream. Inside the box, the water is pure. There's no equation for it there.

I have to remember to look at the box, to imagine its roof raised, the smell of its loam a balm, the shape of joy a seedling leaning into light. Even in the dark, the shape holds firm. No words pass between my joy and me.

The box's humid roof melts paper, but only after headlines have outlived their usefulness. It turns to art inside the box.

As a child, he wrote a world history from A to E. The archives were known to hide seeds and dusty butterfly wings. Something fertile was stuck between files detailing criminal acts. His archive a box, the box he carried across the room, papers spilling off like one-winged doves.

I started a novel one summer, only later seeing how object became symbol, how my fictions failed. It made me blush, though only I had the key. That wasn't a form of joy, but of ambivalence. I told a friend that was my central emotion. We talked again yesterday, decades folded between our fingers like dog hair stuck to a cushion. The dog knows about my joy; yesterday she nestled against a friend riven by grief. Friend smiled.

Neither is that joy, that slight updraft from grieving, the stairway a prop for heart and back. But I look at her now through the window. When we touch eyes, we make seratonin between us. *Eat the rainbow*, a shopping bag hanging from a nail in an abandoned house reads. Its colors dissolve on contact, or what we take to be the touch of eye to horizon.

I turn from the television to my terrarium, releasing a conspiracy into its box of warm air. The murmuration of the mob fades into clock tick and faint hammering. We look at one another like child and fish, or like sun and wooden floor through window. Remember to take pain in with your breath, then let it out again as joy.

Five or Six Perfections

20 June 2022

Each of us has only five or six ideas. My perfection is time. The present is a glowing drop I keep sliding away from. I try to read the forest floor as if it were an alphabet consisting of frying pans.

Each of us has only five or six ideas. Throw them in a field like bones and see what creatures come to smell them as they rot. The boneyard is not idea, but burial site. Perfection of place.

Each of us has only five or six ideas. They wiggle like a magician's plates, defying physics until he sweeps across the stage. Today, mine hide from me, like my dog beneath a blanket. Five or six times she howled in her sleep.

Each of us has only five or six ideas. Either we husband them or we do not. Either we're frugal or profligate. Our early work might have been enough. But in this lateness, light.

Each of us has only five or six ideas. He begins every poem with the weather. The weather is bad today, so wait five or six more. Take notes on each day's conditions, as they shift. The weather is visible idea, unless it's just the weather.

Each of us has only five or six ideas. We breathe them in and out, out and in, wondering at repetition as a state of being, then being again. You cannot breathe the past, one says, though I filter it through this tense, counting toward the future past.

Forgive Us Our Trespasses

25 June 2022

On the armrest of a couch, just above the old golf trophy, I found a Ronald Reagan photo book. He wears a cowboy hat and smiles at the ceiling.

On a broken windshield on a broken car, I found a gnome whose hands spread wide: "This is how much I love you," it read. One ornamental eye was missing.

On the filthy bathroom sink, a bottle of blue mouthwash.

Next to another old house, a ruined piano, keys and strings bent, lying on the ground amid the weeds. I title my photo "4' 33"," which gets checked into a show as "four feet, 33 inches."

The inventory of abandonment includes our and our mothers' wars. It's a lineage, violence. It frames our biographies, the opening diagrams of Russian novels, the day after Roe v. Wade was overturned. Turn over the loam, seed it with tears. We walk toward the explosion, knowing it will happen. "But they said it was settled law."

My mother wept at military cemeteries in Europe, but later she drank her tears. Rust ate away at the scaffolding of her grief. Rust grew between feeling and expression, until they lost track, like long-ago roommates. No phone call brought them back together. Only the arbitrary remained.

We compare the numbers of our D&Cs, laugh nervously at their criminality, as of yesterday. "Take your dogma off my daughter." Mine writes to say what a terrible day, something about Texas. Stay in a blue state, I advise her. Red is for anger; blue is for grief.

To make an inventory is to organize, to take account, to learn the history of your things. An inventory exists in the present; there is none for what I had ten years ago, or will have ten years hence. It's the math we do around our feelings when they attach to things. When I count my losses, I see stuffed animal, rusted car, a scattering of ashes. No longer objects, they are now fake news.

The Wrought Urn

27 June 2022

She drank her tears. Mine sit on the edge of the cliff, feet dangling, breath in the throat, but they won't fall. I dream my thirst.

She drank her tears, feared a final break, her frail spine turned toward gravity, face set hard. I left mine at an Ash Wednesday service in Charlottesville. A friend left hers at a cafe after a movie. He left his in our kitchen. My son left his with one cat. Home is an elastic that sobs around you. It tries to breathe, like ribs apart from lungs.

I am suffocated by the news. It's not news, but reversion to the mean world.

Never have sentences seemed so literal. Sentence as chain, as length of punishment. Ancient Greek accents are like "goats chained to a post," my teacher said.

A shopping mall was bombed in the Ukraine. A shopping mall was the site of a mass shooting in the USA. Violence rhymes, though we think of rhyme as ease, not peril. We are rhyming us to death.

Dickinson's failure to rhyme is like an IED. The track of her poem breaks like Highway 11 during the eruption. She hadn't seen volcanoes, but I have, and heard them rumble and crack. A parking lot fell in the pit, almost flat enough for pickle ball.

Her daily photo from Ukraine remains the same: tall apartment blocks taken from one similar. She writes that she hasn't slept much. Explosions in the distance. But she'll be all right. She needs some likes. I give her one.

If a word means, it consoles. That's what I used to think. Kipukas live on lava fields; they're framed. Life like a surprise. When I watched McCartney (in bits) at Glastonbury, I remembered what joy resembles. Assembled like legos, logos.

Take a soft shield to battle. Let it give, in and back. Don't get angry; respond only with love.

Erasures

15 July 2022

We witness after before before: the bent, ruined carriage where a woman and her daughter were in the photograph we see now. Photograph from above, mother of daughter, carriage beside them. We don't see what the words record: body parts in the street. We see only objects. Stand-ins, voters by proxy, shareholders of a walk down a street somewhere in the Ukraine. It must have been sunny.

Both photographs are of things we don't see, but know were present. Images of absence: the stained white wall between photographs. It's at once what's censored and most there. "Cause of death still unknown" in at least three instances. The disappearance of poets goes without saying because our mouths are taped shut. Silence is more of a temptation than speech.

"A womb serves no purpose to a woman," the elected official opines. "It's a sanctuary." Her body has already been exploded into pieces, those that are hers and those that are sacred. A man put his child in a dumpster in Illinois to protect him from bullets. The dumpster-womb held the boy until the rain ended. It was a sacred space.

Is it worse to play the Uvalde audio, or to erase it? We know children were screaming, but somehow not hearing what we know absolves us of suffering. Our suffering, not theirs. They were trapped in a classroom-box as now in silence. A cop is seen inside the school, holding his big gun, smiling.

Laughter is the explosion of smiling. Links have been located between terror and humor. Kafka laughed, while the Mona Lisa smiled. Civil defense sirens are public laughter designed to protect us from the weather or each other. What we fail to see will hurt us tomorrow. Communications systems were migrated so that only the relevant texts went missing. A lousy excuse is a veil over excresence.

There is such pleasure in words. Dydasko means to teach. True and Caprice Dydasco play soccer.

Mapping the Field

31 July 2022

You can find me behind my thoughts, in the back of the warehouse. A refrigerated truck spews condensation into the alley, like talk balloons without words. Silence is like that, always suggesting, seldom delivering, taking the middle spaces between idea and deed, where Greek sentences so often sit, trying to balance the two, knowing them part of an ethical conundrum that even a cave can't fix. You can find my feelings there, if you care to look, though of late I've been hiding them again from the workplace I left behind. But that was a literal leaving, like my son's this Wednesday, not the remnant trail advertising a perfect mantra to heal your aches and pains. We advertise our lacks, the holes in our texts, the oranges that fill our hearts too full to remain unheard. If this is not poetry, what is it?

Another Russian assault on eastern Ukraine. Everyone is encouraged to leave. Leave-taking as trigger, whether forced or not. But at the end of a missile there's more to your trauma than absence or loss of person (including self) to time's flows. He suspects we don't have polar bears at our zoo, and I laugh at the thought. But we saw a motorcade for the new tiger the other night, filing past Ala Moana, shopping mall that fronts the Pacific Ocean, as if that were possible to do.

Symptoms of trauma: pecking away at your laptop, plucking for hours at a ukelele, beating back the clouds from the Japanese movie about the films we make after our deaths. Choose one moment to direct. Pick your actors carefully. Turn the camera's crank, making that sound, as of fast, high-pitched train tracks. Gaze into the camera, as if it might keep you on the other side of the clouds, even as you know it will not. Is there audience for your film? Does it matter if the reviews come back negative, or come back not at all?

And then you met me. And then I met you. The *and* does not add one thing to another, but suggests a turn in time. Because if *if* had supplanted *and*, then we'd not be here, would we? Suit up for your morning walk with the dog. Palms are crackling. We think the wind is blowing the right way.

Wings (not the band)

13 August 2022

A pause for the heat. A pause for being not sick or dying. A pause for others, who are. May my angel be quieter than these blue machines that slice the air like serrated knives. Imagine if they were attacking you, my father said during Gulf War 1, how terrifying that would be. May my angel be not of anger but of mercy. May I not see the shadow of a plane over me, but an ordinary bird of ordinary pitch looking for an ordinary worm, me.

Some days his skin is as sensitive as a top secret document; you could dust it for prints, but there would still be the mystery of how it got here, locked away in a basement out of the sunshine, put to bed in a leather box. I wish I could make characters to fit my ideas, but I'm reduced to finding them on the local sidewalks and roads winding through the cemetery. Often, they don't fit, but that's what makes them so interesting, reverse allegorical misfits who hold mirrors to our faces. The woman in a MAGA hat offering solace to an immigrant woman. The abuser who loves my dog. You cannot purify purity, but you can make hay out of approximation.

The store was closed for air raid in Kyiv. The highway was closed for a terrorist in Ohio. The violent and the dead are inconveniences we're obliged to live with. Destruction is either a crime or an art. We confuse them like rabbits and vases.

My favorite tree breaks out in a thick black sap that runs down its light brown trunk. Other spaces open where the bark folds back, revealing glyphs in the shape of a leaping animal or a stylized man. They'd mean something, if someone intended it. I could spend a day seated beneath this tree, but the mosquitoes are too thick.

When my teacher asks me to see the images on my closed eye lids, I see darkness only. Last night I dreamed of bright yellow wings. Where they took me I can't say, though like a small child I proclaimed the butterfly yellow. "I've been in kindergarten for six days!" a neighbor boy told me. Pride begins in sweetness.

We see the Russian tank through the sights of a javelin. The tank rampages down a narrow road between tall trees. Dragoning fire from its back, it spins around and stops dead. Men the color of the tank emerge from its hatch. They run.

A dragonfly's wing resembles a stained glass window set on the earth. A drop of black sap turns green for the camera lens, which holds its viscous drop up to the internet. Each walk is a sequence of pictures taken and not taken. An old woman sits in a chair beneath the mountain, leaning over to a grave, adjusting something gently. Her son walks toward her, phone before face, having brought her here in a car. I'll remember her as one not taken.

A Broken Pot Repeats

27 August 2022

Not to make the war a decoration, as it fades from the front view, like men and boys leaping from a bridge in Hilo, framed by the bus's windshield, its fare altar. All I see some days is suffering. The self-love of selfies, professional announcements, the pain of succeeding when you think yourself unworthy. But that's hardly the loss of limb or nation, though it might start there. The Israeli psychologist teaches mindfulness to refugees. Just ten minutes of peace: vacation from exile, that horrible tourism. A small child sang us from Hilo to Honolulu yesterday, "Mommy" and "Daddy" to the tune of happy birthday, occasional shrieks. On the other side of the aisle, an Asian woman with white hair clutched a bunch of bright red anthuriums. The couple next to me were going to visit Pearl Harbor. The man hated Jim Jordan and people who push ahead and out of the plane. At the gate, I sat between a woman speaking Samoan into her phone, and another woman speaking the language of Frail Parent on hers.

From her window in Kyiv she sees large apartment buildings; each day she takes a short walk to work out, drinks her war coffee, and sends out tweets. The streets of Kyiv are nearly as lively as those of Paris, 1915. Giddy and dark with the knowledge of suffering nearby. If they don't watch their televisions, and we do, we find ourselves closer to the conflict than they are. (Leave out the air raids.) Watch the sunrise over the caldera and up Mauna Loa, I tell the tourists. "We're going to see the volcano now," they say that mid-afternoon at Lava Rock Cafe.

Lilith's head rests in the crack of the couch, eyes closed, ears up. Yesterday, two young women, one in pink the other in white, got out of a white Chevy SUV and asked to pet "him." They wore name-tags that marked them as "Sisters." I declined to hear about Our Lord Jesus Christ, but wished them well. On our way back, we saw them with another woman, another dog.

Kintsugi unfractures the pot with gold. You can still see the break, but it's more beautiful than the unbroken. They'll switch out the wilting flowers soon, because there's no fixing them. I prefer dead hydrangeas to the loud blue ones, the lace of brown leaves so delicately traced. These days I remember places by the photographs I took, or left behind. I want to remember what happened by playing it again, because otherwise it breaks.

This is 64

10 October 2022

Is aesthetics anxious? Must my walks be pedestrian? To be readable is to be ordinary; to be ordinary is all there is. It's not just the extremities that hurt; the distinction between pain and suffering signifies a gap between ouch and ache. Missiles hit Kyiv last night, return on a destroyed bridge. Watch one truck come through, the next one lost in a ball of flame. Blood's stickiness stays as grief's remainder.

Neighbor P (as my phone calls him) rails against heaps of garbage at the curb, leaflets at the door. He'll throw them all away. I try to distinguish between "solicitation" and "free speech," but he says we agree to disagree before I can disagree again. He can't believe anything. His mother listens to Christian radio. That's propaganda, but so is everything else. That's our disagreement, not on the facts but on how to find them. Whether they even matter, matter being a form of existence. In this hierarchy, fact is no pillar, but post-truth is nowhere near as much fun as surrealism. Lacks a charge. The line about fuses is out-dated, Bryant says, after I opine that coming home at quarter to three is not true to age 64. Maybe in my dreams you'll leave a crack in the imaginary door. Real toads live on the stairs outside.

Anger writ large is a missile that hits a national university. We do that more slowly in this country. After a pregnant woman jumped in front of a bread truck, UPS told the others to keep working. This was in Louisville. Next time, put up a safety net. Where safety equals life, where life means we breathe, where breath denotes a body. As we get older, embodiment gets more deliberate. I am conscious because I decay.

Two Buddhist teachers sat in a garden. One to the other said, "imagine, they call that a tree!"

Time the Illiterate

14 October 2022

Cat a cat a category. Dog a dogma. Pet the petard. Whole words as fragments, pieces as holes in a blanket. Dog puts nose through hole. All we see is black nose, blue blanket. Blue blanket thrashes when I finish granola bar, place green foil on the floor. It's not the way sound generates meaning, but how meaning generates sound. Small words are best, like mosquitoes on the arm of a sentence, making it itch. Hairs stand there without standing. Hair looms: over or as machine? The fabric made therefrom might be scarf, if we wore them, or turtle neck if it were cold. Cat fur makes turtle neck soft. Shell games go on without. In listening to him read, I suddenly heard some tics, sound stitches across poem fabric. The era of flags flags. The noun verb thing continues apace. We pace to fit the vowels in their slots. Some call it meditation.

Shooter is category. Shooter is 15 years old. Shooter wandered a path by the creek; he went a-shooting. Jogger, guy going to work, his brother. Wore camo. Camus restated: the question not of suicide but of other-murder. She died not by her hand but by another's. He awakened from a dream of wet concrete, his hands gray and stiff. If we dream of concrete, does our dream then set?

Ashes to ashes. Mine can't get out the door, whether cat or mother ash. Mother is category. Mother loved dogs. Mother was dogmatic, something of a prude. But then shone her eyes about the plugs and sockets, male and female. What one to another does, she said. Florida, its first lady claims, is a free state. Was its name ugly, or pristine? Piscines by the beach waste water. Waste water plants redeem it, except when it rains. All of us love the picayune. A White woman screamed the n-word at a Black woman and a White man reeled. It is just a word. No word is, on its own, just.

The real reels. Realism's an eel, a lissome one. Snakes through cracks, code cracks. Knee and back. Crack. Crack reporter, at 23, breaks stories like raw noodles. Starchy, too. You are not your accent. You are not a spice. You are the dot that moves across the screen, marking the DMZ between then and then. Now is too hard to find, not yet a hand in concrete. My face is young, but my hands are old. They are turning into mine.

A Metaphor is For

16 October 2022

A large piece of palm is trapped in a neighbor's yarn spiderweb. Leaves pirouette from the webs of Volcano; this yarn web signals stasis. Oh web without maker, what do you mean to tell us? Ben hates metaphor because it takes us away from what is tangibly here. I respond they also make real toads. Not that I have any proof, but I believe it's so, and that's enough in this climate. Nor do I think metaphor markets in religion, though webs have been so used, not to denote death traps, but as images of connection. If I were to dream a train whose tracks were iron only in the direction it traveled, as what it left behind melted like sap into the trellis's cross hairs, I might have explained something. Then again, explanation's over-rated. To explain is neither to praise nor defame, posit nor deposit. It's a neutral space, like the old Walter Cronkite. One can believe in nets without knowing what they contain.

Russia pulls men off the streets to fight in the Ukraine, taking men from prison. They hunt men to hunt other men. The sidewalk might be a trap, or a rural road. The trap is violence front-dated, once their week of training is complete. Your debt is men who are still alive, then so quickly spent. In the poem, the bridegrooms are already dead. To marry a dead man is an act of back-dated faith. I loved the man so I must love his corpse. The beauty of our net gets shredded inside the thought of men falling into theirs. Pyramid scheme that collapses under the weight of the trap itself, if it were an idea. The man's mother was sent to Siberia; her sister survived the death camps. The first woman left food on her plate; the second one couldn't bear to leave a single crumb.

To pull a shark or a turtle from a net. To save a man from dying and then, handed an award by the police, to eviscerate them. To take your moment cold, knowing it's there. The eucalyptus tree near the swimming pool has trapped a gecko in its goop. It's a web that's only a trap, perhaps. When I went back, ants had found the gecko, covered it with bodies and legs, dim against black sap, visible only where the tree was dry. Neither tree nor ants intended to catch the gecko and consume it. This was not design, but accident, netting similar result. If dementia is surrealism brought to earth, then this tree's sap-covered roots are demented. Tomorrow the gecko will have been forgotten, by tree and by ant and by me. To eat is to forget.

—*for Ben Friedlander*

On Liking

17 October 2022

Be the first to like this because liking is good. The first is a form of being, but only in the future past, when I will have remembered clicking. Parse the difference between a red heart and a blue thumb's up. Match your pay scale to your quantity of likes. Even dislikes (which don't exist) will do, because they mean someone's eyes paused, finger moved, synapse fired. We can see the first two, but not the third, as mind is as invisible to eye as it is to mind. To think is to spelunk, but there's no time for it. The surface seems so much more reasonable, more "relatable," more of a piece with our shards of hours and minutes, pre-destroyed by the judgment system. If I put up a selfie and you like it, are you liking me or my photograph or the fact that I've offered it to you without knowing who you are, unless you like it?

A problem arises in liking tweets from the Ukraine. Kamikaze drones that kill garner as many likes as any day in the park. In which case "like" stands in for "I've noticed this and want you to know it's so." Shorthand of shorthand. He called her Shorty in the elevator. Short greetings pierce the shafts. One cave had a clothes rack across the back, hangers arrayed but lacking anything to hold. Not an allegory of detachment, but of not-having, though it might also be seen as photograph only. Composition over subject. Affect over fact. What we see and feel more than our history. This can go both ways: I can cherish the memory of a feeling without remembering its instance, or I can operate according to my gut, and my gut doesn't like you. My gut might send you to Delaware or Illinois with other migrants. I care only for those I know, not those I stand beside on the subway or those who are as abstract as the fear they engender in me. Caravans of abstractions come north, when needed to swing some votes. You don't see it, because you're too busy liking something else, like a flower because that is what photographs are for. That's not a poem! she wrote to me, because the photograph was of ugliness. But a trapped green gecko on a rainbow eucalyptus, its head threaded to the tree by sap string, is beautiful. Deal with it.

Many have stopped liking; they resign, get off the platforms, develop private lives or whatever passes for private these days. When the boy dropped dead beetles on a couple making love below, they knew nothing of it. They had chosen a semi-private space for a semi-public act, and this was the thanks they got for it. Someone once rated my friendship with her by making two columns, one of what was worth keeping, the other what was not. I was astonished.

Imagine a Word

26 October 2022

Imagine an I and an It, where It is also Thou. The short word pierces sense. What I am to the word is what the word is to the thing it names. We are subjects to each other, which is not to say subjected to, but real in the way spirit is.

Imagine a word that means what it says. Beauty as direction, bluntness even. A stroke pierces mind, but takes only words away. Four hours later, the word returns, pretending nothing had happened, wagging its tail.

Imagine knowing the name of your neighbor at the next desk, asking her what she ate for breakfast, what kind of toothpaste she uses. Think of that as a key to incorporation, not in the sense of finance but of feeling.

What we thought was true is now imagined, though perhaps we imagine that. Depends on whose subject you were, which drinking fountain spouted for your mouth, on which train car you sat. When imagination is only another form of forgetting, let it go.

Imagine a mode of realism that does not involve black lung or mass shootings or melting glaciers. You'll need to get close, so close the dead gecko dissolves into the bright greens and oranges of a gum trees broken skin. It feels like fiction, but it's a clear view.

The pun on spirits breaks a rule. Right speech is not fascist. You can utter the same sentence and have it mean 1) the truth or 2) a lie. It's more than tone shifts, more than punctuation that turns the lens's dial. Hear with clarity; turn off auto-tune.

The week between my mother's birthday and the day my father died must be accident, however inscribed on my inner calendar. My daughter reminds me to take my mother's ashes to Virginia, to place them on the same shelf as my father's. She thinks a lot about the ashes, which sit in our closet, apart from my sight.

Can ashes sing? Can something so impalpable as song emerge from something so inert? What is the material of song? The immaterial of the ashes, which resembles nothing but other ashes.

In *Babylon Berlin*, a young woman is tricked into assassinating the man who hates Nazis. This is an ethical problem with a bomb attached. She was shown a piece of paper that proved her victim had ordered her boyfriend shot. The flyer was passed to her by a Nazi pretending to be a Communist. At show's end, she can no longer pretend to be a young woman.

She had not thought *Cabaret* has so much to offer us. Men in masks, their arms raised in Nazi salutes, stand on an overpass in LA, their banners anti-semitic. The proudest white supremacist is not white. The words for this are what?

Acknowledgments

With love to Bryant, Radhika and Sangha, Anne, Lilith, Thurney, Maeve and Claude.

With thanks to Deborah Meadows, Leonard Schwartz, cris cheek, Valerie Coulton. Atis Puampai for the photography exercises, and for instigating my final project for his class on O`ahu and Hawai`i Island roadside memorials.

This book was written beside Yaraslava Antipina's #warcoffee twitter feed. Another influence was Yevgenia Belorusets War Diary on ISOLARII. I have since discovered work from Ukraine on Pina Piccolo's wonderful literary site, thedreamingmachine.com

Early drafts were put on my blog. Several sections were published in *Chants de la Sirène*. Many thanks to Laura Hinton for her continued support of my work and that of so many others. Her own poetry and thinking are inspirations to me, as well.

Thank you to David Weiss for your early confidence in the manuscript, and to the editors at Spuyten Duyvil (which publishes poetry and prose in translation from Ukraine) for making it into a book.

Volodymyr Zelenskyy: you are an inspiration.

SUSAN M. SCHULTZ lives, writes and takes photographs in Hawai`i, on O`ahu and Hawai`i Island. An emerita professor of English at the University of Hawai`i-Mānoa, she founded Tinfish Press and was its editor for 22 years. Her books of poetry/prose include *Dementia Blog* and "She's Welcome to Her Disease": *Dementia Blog, Vol. 2* from Singing Horse Press; several volumes of *Memory Cards* (Singing Horse, Talisman among them); *I Want to Write an Honest Sentence* (Talisman); *Meditations: Dec. 2019-2020* (Wet Cement); *I and Eucalyptus* (Lavender Ink); *Lilith Walks* and *More Lilith Walks* (BlazeVox). She wrote *War Diary* during the first year of the Russia/ Ukraine War.

www.ingramcontent.com/pod-product-compliance
Lightning Source LLC
Chambersburg PA
CBHW021328060726
47591CB00006B/1917

* 9 7 8 1 9 6 9 9 0 0 1 3 6 *